GAME DAY

GET READY FOR A BASKETBALL GAME

by Emma Carlson Berne

Consultant: Beth Gambro
Reading Specialist, Yorkville, Illinois

BEARPORT
PUBLISHING

Minneapolis, Minnesota

Teaching Tips

Before Reading

- Look at the cover of the book. Discuss the picture and the title.
- Ask readers to brainstorm a list of what they already know about basketball games. What can they expect to see in this book?
- Go on a picture walk, looking through the pictures to discuss vocabulary and make predictions about the text.

During Reading

- Read for purpose. Encourage readers to think about preparing for a basketball game as they are reading.
- Ask readers to look for the details of the book. What needs to happen before the big game?
- If readers encounter an unknown word, ask them to look at the sounds in the word. Then, ask them to look at the rest of the page. Are there any clues to help them understand?

After Reading

- Encourage readers to pick a buddy and reread the book together.
- Ask readers to name two things from the book that a player does to get ready for a basketball game. Find the pages that tell about these things.
- Ask readers to write or draw something they learned about basketball.

Credits:
Cover and title page, © Wlg/Shutterstock and © pedalist/Shutterstock; 3, © baona/iStock; 5, © SerrNovik/iStock; 7, © Brian Díaz/Adobe Stock; 8–9, © Hispanolistic/iStock; 10, © AlexLMX/iStock; 11, © Elenilou/Adobe Stock; 13, © niktalena/Shutterstock; 15, © Ladanifer/iStock; 16–17, © South_agency/iStock; 18–19, © monkeybusinessimages/iStock; 21, © FatCamera/iStock; 22T, © domoyega/iStock; 22M, © domoyega/iStock; 22B, © domoyega/iStock; 23TL, © kali9/iStock; 23TM, © Ababsolutum/iStock; 23TR, © SDI Productions/iStock; 23BL, © HRAUN/iStock; 23BM, © FatCamera/iStock; and 23BR, © FatCamera/iStock.

Library of Congress Cataloging-in-Publication Data

Names: Berne, Emma Carlson, 1979- author.
Title: Get ready for a basketball game / by Emma Carlson Berne ;
  Consultant: Beth Gambro ; Reading Specialist, Yorkville, Illinois.
Description: Bearcub books. | Minneapolis, Minnesota : Bearport Publishing
  Company, [2024] | Series: Game day | Includes bibliographical references
  and index.
Identifiers: LCCN 2023001372 (print) | LCCN 2023001373 (ebook) | ISBN
  9798888220559 (library binding) | ISBN 9798888222515 (paperback) | ISBN
  9798888223703 (ebook)
Subjects: LCSH: Basketball--Juvenile literature. | Basketball--Training--Juvenile literature. | Sportsmanship--Juvenile literature. | Athletes--Health and hygiene--Juvenile literature.
Classification: LCC GV885.1 .B45 2024 (print) | LCC GV885.1 (ebook) | DDC
  796.323--dc23/eng/20230111
LC record available at https://lccn.loc.gov/2023001372
LC ebook record available at https://lccn.loc.gov/2023001373

Copyright © 2024 Bearport Publishing Company. All rights reserved. No part of this publication may be reproduced in whole or in part, stored in any retrieval system, or transmitted in any form or by any means, electronic, mechanical, photocopying, recording, or otherwise, without written permission from the publisher.

For more information, write to Bearport Publishing, 5357 Penn Avenue South, Minneapolis, MN 55419.

Contents

Let's Play! 4

On the Court 22

Glossary 23

Index 24

Read More 24

Learn More Online 24

About the Author 24

Let's Play!

I throw the ball.

Swish!

It goes into the net.

Let's play basketball!

My **coach** showed me how to shoot a basket.

I learned how to **dribble** and pass, too.

Tomorrow is game day.

I am ready!

I go to bed early before my game.

This helps me get lots of sleep.

I wake up with energy.

A healthy breakfast gives me energy, too.

I have toast and peanut butter.

Yum!

I fill up my water bottle.

Then, it is time to get dressed.

I pull on my shorts and **jersey**.

I put on my basketball shoes.

At the **court**, I do **stretches** with my team.

This helps us get our bodies ready to play.

Time to warm up!

We pass the ball.

Then, we shoot at the basket.

The game begins.

Our coach tells us our **positions**.

I sit out first.

I cheer for my team while I am on the bench.

Then, it is my turn to play.

My friend passes me the ball.

We run down the court.

I love basketball!

On the Court

Every player has a job on the basketball court. Here are some basketball positions.

A center plays in the middle of the court. They try to make baskets.

A forward also tries to make baskets. They play all over the court.

A guard dribbles and passes the ball.

Glossary

coach the person who teaches and leads a sports team

court a place where basketball is played

dribble to bounce a basketball while moving

jersey a shirt worn by a player in a sports game

positions the special jobs each player has on a team

stretches ways of moving the body to pull muscles longer

Index

breakfast 10
cheer 18
coach 6, 18
energy 8, 10
jersey 12
stretches 14
team 14, 18

Read More

Leed, Percy. *Basketball: A First Look (Read about Sports).* Minneapolis: Lerner Publications, 2023.

Omoth, Tyler. *Basketball Fun (Sports Fun).* North Mankato, MN: Capstone Press, 2021.

Learn More Online

1. Go to **www.factsurfer.com** or scan the QR code below.
2. Enter **"Basketball Game"** into the search box.
3. Click on the cover of this book to see a list of websites.

About the Author

Emma Carlson Berne lives with her family in Cincinnati, Ohio. Horseback riding is her favorite sport.